## Dedication

To my darling Abby.

## Credits

All photos by Stan Tekiela

Illustrations by Kathie Kemp

Cover and book design by Jonathan Norberg

10 9 8 7 6 5 4 3

**Do Beavers Need Blankets?**
Copyright © 2015 by Stan Tekiela
Illustrations copyright © 2015 by Kathie Kemp
Published by Adventure Publications
An imprint of AdventureKEEN
310 Garfield Street South
Cambridge, Minnesota 55008
(800) 678-7006
www.adventurepublications.net
All rights reserved
Printed in China
ISBN 978-1-59193-467-7

# Do Beavers Need Blankets?

by Stan Tekiela

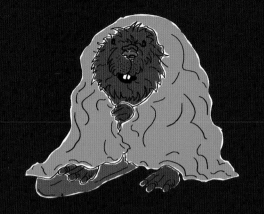

## Do beavers need blankets when they sleep?

Believe it or not, beavers need to go swimming just to get into bed! The entrance to their lodge is underwater, but their fur is so thick that it keeps them warm and dry. They sleep in their cozy lodges during the day.

## Not exactly, but they do have warm fur coats.

# Do coyotes cuddle?

Baby coyotes are born in a dry underground den. Dens can be pretty cold, so when the pups are born they need to snuggle with their siblings and mother to stay warm. When they grow up, coyotes sleep outside, tucked under the protective branches of a tree or beneath other shelter.

Cuddling is what baby coyotes do best!

# Do squirrels snack in bed?

Sometimes squirrels do snack in bed. They sometimes carry acorns or other food back to their dens where they can take their time and enjoy the snack. They may bring other foods to bed, too. During winter they may seek the shelter of their nest to eat and get away from cold winter air. In summer, they sleep in a special leaf nest, called a drey nest, which they make just for sleeping.

## Yes, sometimes they do snack in bed.

# Do porcupines use pillows?

Even a baby porcupine is prickly. Its back and tail are covered with sharp quills that protect it from predators. But predators aren't the only ones that have to worry about the sharp quills: baby porcupines need to be careful or they can get poked by one of their mother's quills.

Porcupines sleep during the day and night in trees; in the winter they seek the shelter of tree cavities to stay warm.

## If a porcupine used a pillow, it'd poke holes in it!

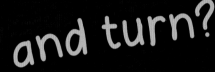

# Do turtles toss and turn?

A turtle sleeps in its shell, so turtles can't really toss and turn. Even if they could, turtles that accidentally get turned over sometimes have trouble standing up, so tossing and turning would be a bad thing. Instead, when turtles sleep, they draw their head and legs deep into their shell and snooze in the safety of their portable home.

# No, turtles sleep in their shells!

# Do opossums use pacifiers?

Baby opossums are only the size of a bean when they are born. They crawl into a pouch on their mother's stomach and start sucking on a pacifier-like part inside the pouch. The babies will nurse from this pacifier for over two months before going outside. When they aren't eating, they are usually sleeping!

## Kind of, but not like a baby's pacifier!

# Do woodchucks dream about chucking wood?

Woodchucks are herbivores and eat only green plants. Dandelions are one of their favorite foods, but they will eat just about any kind of flower. So if they dream about food, they probably dream about flowers! Woodchucks sleep in underground burrows all night and half the day.

They don't actually chuck wood but might dream about fresh, tasty flowers.

sleeps all night and half the day

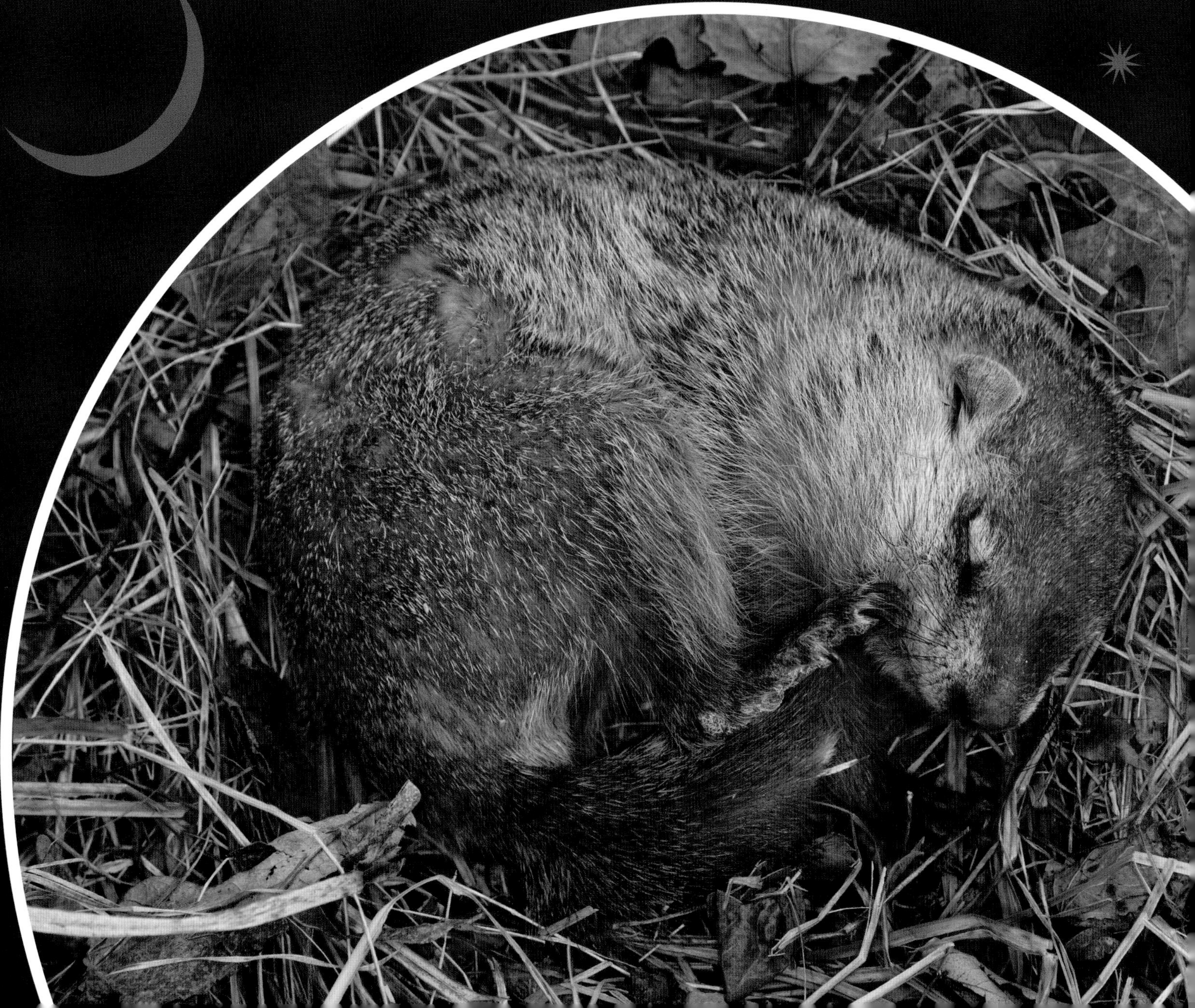

# Do cougars catnap?

When they aren't hunting mice or meowing for food, house cats sleep a lot. So do cougars, which share a lot in common with their smaller cousins. Just like house cats, cougars sleep on and off during the day and night but tend to be slightly more active at night. But don't try to pet one!

Yes, just like house cats!

# Do snakes shut their eyes to sleep?

Snakes are some of the few animals that don't have eyelids. Instead of eyelids that can open and close, their eyes are covered with special clear scales that stay in place, so even when they are fast asleep, usually in areas with some sort of cover, snakes can't close their eyes. So don't have a staring contest with a snake—it will win every time!

## No! They don't even have eyelids!

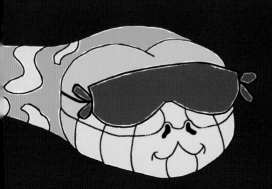

# Does a moose sleep on a mattress?

Moose live deep in the forest and when it's time to rest or sleep, they choose a soft, natural mattress. A moose's mattress is a thick layer of soft mosses and plants. These hold a lot of moisture, helping to keep the moose cool. A moose mattress also keeps mosquitoes and other biting insects away. Moose lie down on a different mattress each time they sleep.

## Yes, but not the kind that you sleep on.

# Do bats sleep in bunk beds?

Baby bats are born in caves, but they are also born upside down! A baby bat's mother hangs upside down, too. The baby clings to its mother for warmth and protection. Unless they are flying, bats do everything upside down, including sleeping. See if you can sleep upside down tonight!

## No, but they do sleep upside down!

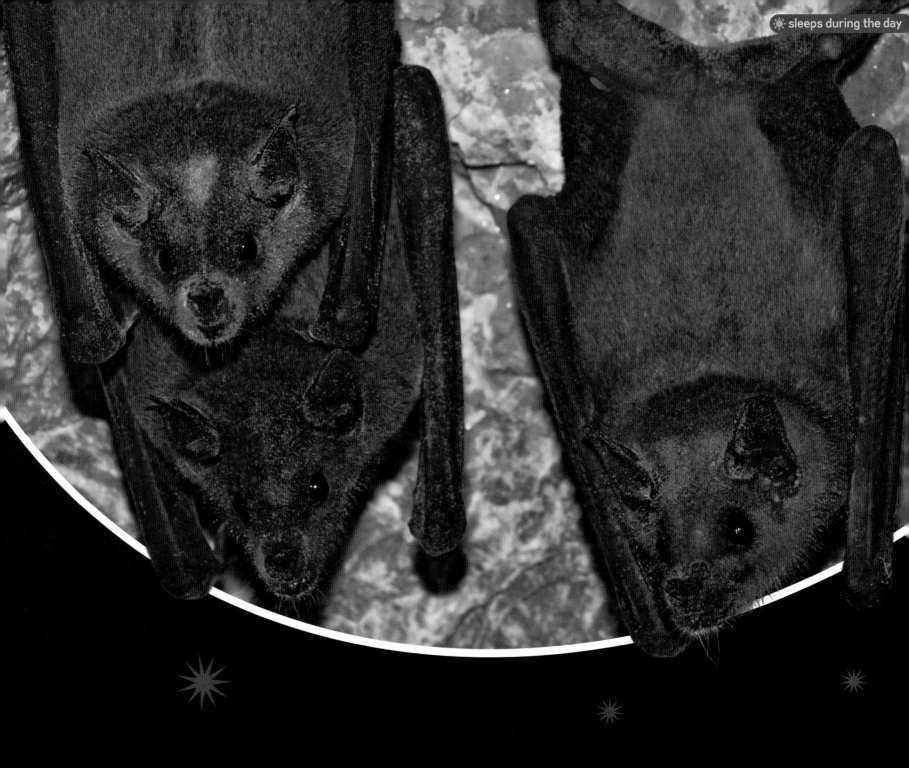

# Do skunks sleepwalk?

Skunks don't sleepwalk, but they are active at night when *you* are sleeping. Skunks sleep during the day in their dens, and it's not rare for campers to hear skunks wandering past tents and campsites at night. But don't worry, skunks won't hurt you. They are just out looking for insects, plants and other tasty foods.

## No, but they do walk around when you're sleeping!

# Do bears sleep with teddy bears?

Mother bears give birth to two, three and sometimes four teddy bear-like cubs during winter. These bears cuddle their brothers and sisters, just like you curl up with your teddy bear. But bear cubs snuggle to survive: they don't have much fur so they need to cuddle to stay warm as they sleep in their cold winter den.

## Yes, but their teddy bears are real!

# Sleepy Questions

## Do critters snore?

Nearly all animals will snore when sleeping. It may not be loud and obvious like with some people, but critters usually make snoring sounds. Snoring comes from air rushing past the soft plate in the back of the mouth, causing vibration. Too bad they don't make any breathe-right strips for critters.

## Do animals dream?

Dreaming is common in all animals. As critters fall into deep sleep, their eyes move around quickly, and they start to dream. Dreaming is often associated with twitching of their whiskers and even their feet and legs, as if they were running. The stage where the eyes are moving is called REM, or rapid eye movement. Believe it or not, this is not the deepest part of sleep. Later when the critter is sleeping really deeply, it doesn't move or twitch at all.

## Do young animals wet the bed?

Most animals don't wet their beds. Studies with white-tailed deer show that deer get up from their beds and move a short distance before urinating. However, some small critters, such as mice, often wet their nests. The medical name for wetting the bed is "nocturnal enuresis."

## Which animals sleep standing up?

Some larger animals, such as white-tailed deer and moose, will sleep standing up, but this is not very common. Even these huge animals will sit down to rest. Many hours are spent lying down, chewing their cud and napping. Some shorebirds sleep while standing on one leg with their bill tucked under a wing. They have the ability to sleep with just half of their brain. For example, they will close their right eye, resting the corresponding left side of the brain. Then they switch eyes to rest the other side of their brain.

## Which animals sleep the shortest time and which the longest?

Many animals sleep much longer than even we sleep. Squirrels, for example, will sleep about 15 hours a day. Snakes sleep about 20 hours a day. The opossum sleeps about 18 hours a day. Bats sleep about 20 hours a day. Felines, such as bobcats and lynx, sleep over 20 hours a day. Bears do a lot of sleeping during hibernation. They may sleep for several days on end, occasionally waking, changing position and then going back to sleep. This can go on for many months. We people sleep about 8 hours at night. When added up, we spend about a third of our lives sleeping. That is about 25 years' worth of sleeping if you live a full, long life.

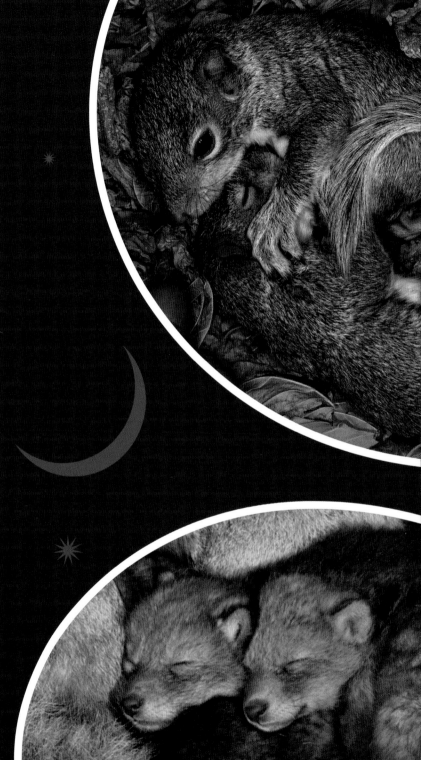

## Do all animals sleep at night or day?

Some animals, like birds, sleep at night while others, such as skunks, sleep during the day. Animals that sleep at night and are active during the day are called diurnal. Critters that sleep during the day and are active at night are called nocturnal.

## How can you tell if an animal is sleeping if it doesn't have eyelids?

Many animals, such as the common loon, have white eyelids, so when they close their eyes it looks like their eyes are actually open. Some reptiles, such as snakes, don't have any eyelids, and so they sleep with their eyes open. They have a clear scale that covers each eye, protecting it. Each time they shed their skin, this cap comes off and is replaced with a new one. Birds have two sets of eyelids and close both when they are sleeping.

## Do animals sleep alone or together?

Many critters sleep together. Animals that live in family units often sleep in a big heap in their dens. Squirrels, woodchucks and mice will all sleep together in their cozy nests. Many more animals sleep alone in their dens. Most birds will sleep alone, but some, such as the black-capped chickadee, will all huddle together in a protected cavity to sleep the night away.

## About the Author

Stan Tekiela is a naturalist, wildlife photographer and author of more than 120 books. He has a biology degree from the University of Minnesota.
Check out his other children's books, *Baby Bear Discovers the World, Critter Litter, The Cutest Critter, Some Babies Are Wild* and *Whose Butt?*